SECOND FLEET BABY

For my mother, Suzanne

SECOND FLEET BABY

NADIA RHOOK

FREMANTLE PRESS

Contents

Susannah of the Sea

Settler Dawns

Federation Pains

Fuss or Fertiliser

Watching *Free Willy* in the Age of Covid-19

SUSANNAH OF THE SEA

Porter, Susannah (Susan) (c. 1790–1835)

Susannah Mortimer (c.1790-1835), the daughter of convict, Susannah Mortimer, was probably born during the voyage of the *Lady Juliana* from Portsmouth to Sydney in 1789-1790. It is thought her father may have been a sailor on the ship, William Screech. Susannah accompanied her mother to Norfolk Island on the *Surprize* in August 1790 and took her stepfather Thomas O'Brien's surname. Her mother had at least eight more children with O'Brien.

Susannah left Norfolk Island with her mother and stepfather on the *City of Edinburgh* in September 1808. George Porter was also on the ship. Susannah and Porter were married at Hobart on 21 November 1808; both signed the register with their mark. The couple had at least seven children. Following her husband's death in 1828 Susannah continued to work the family farm.

Susannah Porter was buried (as Susan Porter) on 7 May 1835 at Glenorchy, Tasmania. Her age was given as 45 and her occupation as 'settler's wife'.

* Information from Michael Flynn, *The Second Fleet: Britain's Grim Convict Armada of 1790* (1993), p 448

[view family tree]

Related Entries in NCB Sites

- Porter, George (husband)
- O'Brien, Susannah (mother)
- O'Brien, Thomas (stepfather)

Life Summary [details]

Alternative Names
- O'Brien, Susannah
- Mortimer, Susannah
- Screech, Susannah

Birth
c. 1790
at sea

Death
6 May 1835
Glenorchy, Hobart, Tasmania, Australia

Cause of Death
unknown

Passenger Ship
- Lady Juliana (1790)

Occupation
- farmer

Key Events
- Second Fleet (1789-90)

Citation details

'Porter, Susannah (Susan) (c. 1790–1835)', People Australia, National Centre of Biography, Australian National University, https://peopleaustralia.anu.edu.au/biography/porter-susannah-susan-31632/text39106, accessed 1 February 2022.

after the First Fleet we made some calculations

versed in the arithmetic of sex

gathered round artisanal tables
we discussed how many is enough to
build a successful colony

the air was tense with possibility

one of us suggested we don't need any
another shook his fist

look! how history trembles when faced with
the undeniable importance of one body reaching for another in the
night

look! how we are prepared to forge an uncertain future
only while doing sums

= the minimum cargo of women

fleet lives

fleet (n.)

from Old English fleotende 'floating, drifting'
later 'flying, moving swiftly'

*Following the First Fleet, the British government handed the business
of convict transportation to private ship owners who had no financial
incentive to keep the prisoners alive until the completion of
the voyage. The death rate of those transported
increased dramatically.*

for you

privatisation felt like
handing over a carefully signed contract and
cases bulging with money

sharp-clawed vultures launched from battle-
frayed shoulders
burdens of responsibility eased

for forty percent of this fleet

privatisation felt like
floating toward a new life before
sinking

feeling through currents and through death how
there's no such thing as peace in the
ocean's unmarked graves

in university I learnt that history is nothing but context

> *the context of this story*
> *is*
> *thick*
> *with criminal women loose*
> *women strategically-beneficial-for-the-colony women*
> *'settler-wife' women*
>
> *women who were free then owned then*
> *free women who dug their heels in against this Act*
> *and that act*
> *women who inherited almost half the world*
> *to sell it to the best-*
> *dressed bidder*

Plymouth

    Rio de Janeiro

        Eora land

           Norfolk Island

        North Atlantic

South Atlantic

Indian Ocean

with each port the chains that

kept them below deck

asking

do you want to spread weeds across another

person's carefully tended garden do you

want to jump overboard and   commune with the

dolphins the plankton   they have language

too   listen   by the

time we step onto Eora land the colony

already

rising up to become the saline

solution within

in one corner of her mind

she's lying on slats on a bed rigid and rectangular enough to be a
plank to be a technology that lets you slide efficiently from smooth
deck to rough ocean she knows how this goes this melting of bone yet
as the pressure builds she doesn't expect to be so angry at the ocean
how
      dare it toss and turn for the sake of tossing and turning how
dare it behave so recklessly while part of her wants to throw her life
away to give in to this energy that does not care where it pushes life as
long as it pushes life she is waiting for the next wave she is all
      clammy skin and crowded thoughts hands pressing into
her palms hands laid on her knees wiping sweat from her head hands
lying pretending this story can only have one ending and when
      she's not angry at the ocean she's angry at the doctor
not because he's floating around her ankles like a dinghy moored on a
serene lake but because he's not angry at the ocean how dare he
      float like that how dare he act like he's saving her when she's
so busy saving herself she is under the next wave now and not sure
which way is up the ocean screaming a string of words that
      sounds like north-south-west-east-up-down-north-west-
up-east-down and she's saving herself this second and that one the
light coming in from every direction she finds a shaft lets the
      light dive beneath her body the voices puncture her
skin reminding her there's still a membrane a stretchy supple organ
separating her life from the rest of life the voices assaulting her ears a
voice in her left
      ear telling her she can do this she has done it
before and a lot of other women have done it too after one hour of
this the light diving into her body turning it to

ripples the anger leading her to consider if she's become
anger himself she starts to see the turning and the tossing as God at
a sailors' party chugging down drink after
drink swinging his arms knowing there's hardly a difference
between freedom and flaunting untameable power and almost as
soon as she forgives the ocean she
meets her daughter this bright ball screaming as if
there's no reason to disguise the shock of entering the world with
its doctors and hands and oceans and planks this ship where every
drop of power has been invited where
a woman holds the ocean in one corner of her mind while
dragging life from the seabed to the surface with another

the midwife

in a tent pitched in a corner of the deck
　　you lit wax candles
　　　　soaked sponges with liquor
　　　　infused hot water with chamomile and hartshorn
　　　　　　pointed her to the stool
　　　　　　held it still while she
　　squatted and her
baby, through gravity, dropped, slimy, into your hands

　　　　　　ignoring the burn playing in the space between warmth and
　　　　　　　　fire travelling along your inner
　　　　wrist, you listened to her eyes, lifted water to her lips, pressed
　　　　sponge to brow for

centuries, back on land, you'd answered to the church letting them
　　know if any mother had killed her child or
　　conducted a heathen ritual with her placenta

　　　　here, far from surveillance and steeples, you
　　　　　helped my ancestor
　　　　　　return to what the doctor would the following day call
　　　　　　　　a 'natural state of good health' as if

　　　　　nature might be separate from knowledge from
　　　sponge from tendon

Screech

sprinting through the velvet protections of night to
    hustle a sheep

      salivating at the thought of mutton while questioned about the
scale of your criminal
          intent the line between guilt and innocence becoming
blurrier than a town's silhouette hours into the passage

    a daughter you call Susannah Mely Screech sliding into
        life via a surface thinly coated with sweat and
          other invisible remnants of desire

    Susannah meaning   lily of Hebrew origin
Mely meaning   song, of Hawaiian origin
      Screech meaning   a way to express how it feels to

    fit a place you've never met inside your abdomen like
conjuring in your mind the distraction of an exotic flower like

      singing a song you love but have never heard like
      squeezing into a single laboured breath the pain of

      sudden growth

at some stage in all this you took a second to
    notice how arching your back lends your life a release, the air
      completing the small
          gap between each of your spine's vertebrae this
        strong chain of brittle
          decisions

the likeliest of cradles

and so
this daughter
claimed life

during an afternoon crammed with
empire's heavy traffic
head pointing in the direction of the metropole
feet toward the starving colony her
lips gaping in the presence of the sail shaking with wind
heart flaring in sync with the opening sky
the ship the likeliest of cradles
a vehicle of compulsory beginning
running on slavery's surplus and promises made
in late-night tussle of sheets moulded with passionate obligations and
half-hearted declarations

a compass pointing toward the
rich gooey placenta-wrapped
engine caked in dried blood

cutting through the certainty of four cardinal directions
through the stench of a project fuelled by men incensed by
the power of seed and women who assisted
them to spread it
there was, for minutes, the nauseating scent of new life

        a lily

floated on a sea of rotting weed
and they paused

not yet sure this can be reduced to a story of life versus death
only sure the timbers were creaking under the
weight of vomit and euphoria

Susannah Mortimer

your baby not born on Country
your baby not born on land
your baby rocked to sleep by the
slippery restless body in which
Common Law struggled to gain a foothold

this prisoner

spreads rumours
> *knowledge is power and evidence*

sulks
> *you can't force someone to be cheerful, or to enjoy your lessons*

shaves her own head
> *it's not punishment if you relish the air on your skull*

practises silence
> *you can't be prosecuted for tucking words between your ribs*

dances naked
> taught to *jig during the voyage for the sake of good health* but
> once landed the jailors came to fear a

> *pride*

> *uncontrollable*

the drive to be a puppet master, at once in her body and
out of it, a game played all the way to the gallows

ey! skin organ, cell cell,

ORGAN   SKIN   EY!

inventing rituals on Eora land

do you remember that time the colony ran
out of candles just a couple of years into the dark of it

you had to take your own bread to dine with
the governor you had to

supply your own bedding from the ship in those days
the only thing the colony provided was absolution the

priest raised his arm to baptise every child called 'illegitimate' like
a soldier waged and armed with holy water

each sprinkle a soul saved
a head anointed with belonging

porphyria and convict mothers

In memory of Mary Wade, who arrived on the Lady Juliana, the same convict ship as my maternal ancestor, and whose descendant is former Prime Minister of Australia Kevin Rudd.

it's said that King George the Third suffered from
a degenerative mental disease called

porphyria

and a month after he was cured, in the spirit of celebration, all
the women on death row had their sentences

commuted

from death to
penal transportation to so-called Australia

sometimes I wonder who else lies awake at night thinking how
we were criminals before we were criminal

the way a mere chemical shift in a king's body has
lead to our existence

the molecular lives of those born into
power, the occasional coincidence of

good health with historic changes of mind

'These women are the great, great grandmothers of
thousands of Australians today.'

skirts raised above knees
   the courtyard humming with
   not very musical noise

light bouncing off a hundred bare arses
   light obeying its own properties
   becoming brighter with each bounce

an artist moving toward the easel by
   signs of disdain
   sin echoing in the priest's order-lined ears

       a saucy lot they are

    no way to distinguish this drop of sauce from that one

in time, these smooth shiny butts will hang, treasured, on gallery walls
   in the courtyard they're formidable, a dam wall

           cheek by cheek beside cheek

SETTLER DAWNS

settler dawns

here, a baby can breathe before her mother's waters break

a black and white map can birth a bloody family
a follicle can take a whole body hostage

at high noon we stand upright and walk with confidence through the
gap between the riverbed and the shooting stars

the church tower is firing up crosses that get wedged in
holy constellations of land

history's potted bricks are whispering *she who comes first will be last*
we flinch, try to keep living as if nothing's happened

we were born when we crawled over ancient seabeds into this scene
strengthened our lungs, and cried

This poem was written in response to the cover of *False Claims of Colonial
Thieves* by Charmaine Papertalk Green and John Kinsella (Magabala Books,
2018). The final words of this poem, 'and cried', are a reference to Ruby
Hamad's *White Tears Brown Scars* (Melbourne: Melbourne University Press,
2019), in which Hamad argues, referencing the path-breaking work of Aileen
Moreton Robinson, that White women have often cried in order to perform
a victimhood that oppresses women of colour and Indigenous women. This
poem also alludes to the history of lung evolution. The lungs of reptiles were
coated with a surfactant. As mammals evolved and adapted to breathing air,
this surfactant became thicker to prevent our lungs from collapsing and to
enable breathing. Taken together, this reminds me that human breath holds
a history of the ocean, as the cry of a White woman, my breath, holds the
history of colonisation. This condition of life can feel inescapable, as if the
effects of history precede its causes.

forebear (noun)

'ancestor,' late 15c., from fore 'before' + be-er

'one who exists';

Originally Scottish.

forbear (verb)

'to abstain,' Old English forberan

'bear up against,

control one's feelings, abstain from, refrain';

Of similar formation are Old High German ferberen, Gothic frabairan

'to endure.'

in her wake

they arrived lips tingling with the promise of capital

Ellen dipped her fingers into the sandy, loved boodja, moved her
free hand to shade her baby's face, and asked James again *is this feasible?*

the critiques have been cutting for fifty years too much
land has been granted to too few people

officers are failing to cultivate the soil her own husband has been
granted more than he can possibly use

our time in this colony moving to the irregular beat of a home front she
woke to hot tea, angst, and news

he sometimes returned with blood and fresh hauntings on his trousers
she fixed them

he'd fought in many battles so he called their work an 'invasion'
she called it 'life', only thirteen when they met and
now she's nineteen

a woman in the language of her law and of her men

at first, we
plunge into the civilising project, buoyed by fast progress we

believe in the power of education a child needs to know their
history to know how kings and queens are divined but

hard work under a hot sun is no more romantic than nursing a baby at
sea with your nipples cracked or teaching children to be gentle
during a protracted war and soon

the violence of it all spilled out of the cupboards and drawers until there was
more mess than you could expect a servant to tidy

we became tired

no-one can sleep through the night while under instructions from
a strict government

Ellen stays for ten years
then returns to the land she came from as the

ship slaps against the Indian Ocean she observes a cluster of buildings
sloping hills sidling up to the open sea like

an ex-lover testing the distance between
two once-tangled bodies she moves

her tongue from the top of her front
teeth down to their pointy tips

     P-earth

holding onto the 'th' for as long as it takes to
infuse the air around her with a small mist of England

noticing how invisible her words must appear to those
swimming in her   Footnote

this poem was written on Whadjuk Noongar boodja about events
that took place on Noongar boodja this

poem is a fictional account of the true story of Ellen Mangles who was the
wife of James Stirling, an England-born soldier and colonist who led the

Pinjarra massacre where Binjareb men, women and children
were killed for living as sovereign people on sovereign Country

Ellen and James married in Guildford, England, on Ellen's sixteenth birthday
after ten years co-colonising Whadjuk boodja

Ellen returned to England

movements beyond history

I was subject to gravity. planet pulled to sun. writer pulled to power. historian bound by authority

see how I tied footnotes round my ankles and pretended it was still easy to walk. only kicking off my references and singing from the soles of my feet to the tips of my mind could help me return to the stories I knew just a few days before this all began. a time when my legs flew higher than my waist without needing to question who would verify the height of my kick

having met Europe at the bottom of so many pages I finally understand that I, too, need release

go on. I dare you to imagine.

it feels like becoming airborne,

an illusory absence of weight

footnote

Name
i. The person you think of when you think of the past.
ii. Ranke. The man whose last name rhymes with rank. The man who decided to make history rigorous because inaccuracies in historical fiction are grossly offensive.[1]

Title
i. Your favourite quote.
ii. The painting you hang in your lounge entrance or above your bed.

Publisher
i. The person who believes that what you think matters.
ii. The person who cares about the future even more than the past.

Place of publication
i. The computer screen lit up with your imagination.
ii. Your favourite park bench.

Date
i. The place you met that person you think of when you think of the past.

---

1. The invention of the footnote is often attributed to Leopold von Ranke, who is often cited as the father of the European discipline of History.

origins

origin (n.)

c.1400 'ancestry, race' from Latin originem
'a rise, commencement, beginning, source, descent, lineage, birth' from
the stem of 'oriri': arise, rise, get up; appear above the horizon

    my sister brought a chick home from school

    we trained the chick to walk up the ruler like this was the steep of her
    dreams

       she grew. wider wings. longer beak. louder chirp.

    one day she swooped my sister   left her cheek red and raw   we
    took her for a trip to the country   my uncle handled her   the rest
    of us stood as spectators in the yard   – or was it the driveway –
    nah there was no difference the road, the drive, the yard

    feathers are

      soft

        feathers are

            spiky the

                feathers   took   flight

  the feathers rested on the drive   pliant foxy trails

*

back in the brown vinyl-rimmed late 80s suburban lounge laughter
bounces off the mushroom carpet

Mum listens loudly from the kitchen   my sister and I coax the
chick up the ruler   'you can do it!'

before the chick arrived I'd wandered outside and across the road to
visit our friends, alone

      it felt good to walk somewhere I wasn't allowed

the neighbour opened the door looked down at me
cried 'what are you doing here?'   I don't remember replying

then, the neighbour carried me back across the road Mum was in
the shower and it took her a while to hear the knocks

held by someone I barely knew, I listened past the hum of falling
water for the sound of approaching steps

*

for the first five years of my life, Mum was the only person who could
understand my mumblings

as an adult, I learn how *mother whales whisper to their babies to
keep predators from eavesdropping* and realise one thing I love
about my mother is she never once told me

to 'speak up'

*

there were always papers on the Big Bang
tucked into the Corolla's back-seat pocket

once a month I tried to read the
dense print the long words hinting at a

world existing simultaneously with trampolines and apple-tree
spaceships and other places that direct you to the edge of the

expanse a human mind can hold

driven through Ballarat streets, I was expanding

grey sky shooting away from the car seatbelts warping all wrapped
around me all not-as-secure-as-it-seemed

later, I zoomed in on the title of the paper
'Why we shouldn't believe in the Big Bang'

Dad explained it was because scientific theories are
susceptible to being proven wrong

Newton was brilliant but his theories aren't as true as Einstein's and
so our origins were models of reality to hold onto for
a Sunday drive

*

the train does the labour of separation

Spencer Street station is like most places on these weekends,
lacking sun, sealing pollution, pushing my head closer to the
secrets of the underground

one weekend we enter a new world, a garden full of animals. Dad
stops to speak with the monkeys. calls them cousin. chats away
with a child in his voice

by night we share bunk beds. two of three stacked exactly as
bookish sisters in a study. before we leave we write a message on the
whiteboard beside an algorithm or a theorem. erasable evidence of
our presence. something to check on when we return next month

Spencer Street is always concrete grey. the train is always on
time but sometimes we miss the 5.08 and walk a block up to
McDonalds for a Happy Meal.

the train always passes the stations in reverse order

Melton Bacchus Marsh Ballan Ballarat

when we return to the place with the garden the world is all above
ground and I forget how it feels to walk with the city pressing on
your suitcase, tunnels closing down your eyes.

in the garden, the world is bigger than the garden. there are
mirrors but no secrets. just a trampoline to jump on and the
question of whether or not I'm already in the sky

FEDERATION PAINS

in the sea closest to where I was born

among long deep times

songs

dances

Boon Wurrung stories of the ice age

a sea rising up and moving onto cultivated land

oysters were

temporarily
(plated in gold and

washed (in

bubbling brooks of champagne and
all the little ones waited in a row) the

time has come) said cajoling hands to
leave the comfort of your shells

the second day came (battered, and stewed, the stuff
of food poisoning and Moreton's plush bays, a

regulation-loving man stood (up and proclaimed the
oysters have gotten) too risky we've got

to find another way to play))   a

cloudy fog fell   ) like a

gathering grey (upon the third day
this is the time (we said) for you to

suck up the ocean in the zone around you
filter our debris

(it's scrumptious)

and after the storm (suggested it might yet pass
without flooding our ceramic plates the time came to

turn our hopes ((upon the hatchery

the crib of limestone was laid   the
scaffold))   of shellfish reefs   300,000 tiny oyster

prospects dropped into the ocean (gently

) like one handles thinly shelled eggs, or sedentary sperm
the excrement of pounds) of ancient flesh

stories that run (heavily salted harvests
through)   historians' waterproof hands

oyster interrupted

early on in the
tour she places
slavery in darkness
and paid labour in
the light

the oyster's life
is interrupted with

the insertion of a seed

the oyster releases
liquid to try to
get it out but
most of the time
it stays there and after 2 or more years

the liquid hardens

and that, folks, makes a
cultured pearl

any guesses
what this one's worth?

a shell covered in
barnacles of the ocean's
bacterium is passed

from open palm to opening palm

pearls
might be the circle of joy herself
or a great asymmetrical disappointment

I look back at the seed, the
abductor muscle the oyster's
thin sensory rim

I squirm in my seat
this is too involuntary for comfort

Broome speak

during the sunset   I pause

the ocean's got something to say to us
maybe it's history speaking or maybe
it's other people's ancestors
hard to say for sure

for a split second
between snapping anniversary selfies and
dodging camels and SUVs that crawl like branded ants across the sand

with every snap of the pinkening sky, the
rocks becoming silhouettes, of picnics, the sand
flecks ingrained in my grandmother's sparkly linoleum kitchen floor

the surfaces getting sharper than the day

Broome Broome
Broom Broom

while the ocean projects across the land to
the carpark, the tourists keep clicking

the middle of history is full of rental cars with their handbrakes on

questions begging in the pearl shop

you look scared! don't worry if you drop one it won't break

what do pearls sound like when they bounce
empty like a ping pong ball
or loaded, like a rock

as you can see these ones – we call them Keshi pearls – yes these are lovely too. Keshi are actually naturally occurring but the market prefers a nice round pearl

since rounder is
less natural when
did rounder become better

now, there are five qualities and I'll be testing you on them at the end of the tour – are you listening?

shape [thumb] size [forefinger] colour [middle finger] complexion [ring finger] lustre [pinky]

once I memorise these will I ever be able to
judge a pearl by another virtue

round   large   white   silent   shiny

'it is not as a woman'
(in memory of Dame Dorothy Tangney, 1907–1985)

it is not as a woman
that I have been elected to this chamber. it is as ~~a citizen~~ an inheritor of
stolen land, and I take my place here with the full privileges and rights
of all ~~citizens~~ settler colonists, and, what is more important, with the full
responsibilities which such a burden of theft entails. I trust that I shall
carry out my duties on this country with every regard for the dignity
and honour of the First Nations people who rule Country in a continent
misleadingly called 'Australia', and also to the Whadjuk Noongar boodja
on which I have the privilege to reside. it is not

as a woman that I have been elected to this chamber. it is

not as a woman that I have been elected to this country. it is not

as a woman that I have been elected to this chamber.

it is not as a woman that I have been occupying this country. it is not as a

woman that I have been elected to this chamber. it is

not as a woman that I have been occupying this chamber. it is

not as a woman that I have become this chamber it is

not as a woman that I become this chamber it is not

as a woman that I become Country it is

as a woman that I wish to

Federation pains (c.1901)

when the nation was born
it was loud

screams echoed through the chambers of Parliament
sharp intakes of expectation counter-balanced long moans of debate

at the sound of each other's contractions the legislators closed their eyes
found solace in matching couplets

our Land, our Lady, breathing high
our Land, our Lady, breathing high

inside, warms puffs of self-government rose to a self-determined future
above talking heads and below the bodies of

'Justice' 'Wisdom' 'Mercy'
hips and waists and breasts lined the ceilings

hourly wiping clean the slate on which
they were writing history lessons

outside, dangerous figures had swapped lungs for megaphones

             perfect equali–   enter Parliam–

                              –he rights – of her sex

with tears, the nation slid out from between temporarily naked legs
a chorus of pleasure sounded for

on this day a flag is raised, a
triumph won, a nation born!

until someone yelled over the thickening crowds

is it a girl or a boy?

and like an emperor parading naked before his subjects
the nation's first question cried out for a tailor

what robe is large enough to cover up a nation born through speech

Waste Land

1. Infertile land.
2. Referring to the title of a poem by English poet T.S. Eliot.
3. A legal category employed by European colonisers to steal
   Indigenous land.

like a poet

Looking into the heart of light, the ~~silence~~
speech, ready to be translated

like the poet I always wanted to be called

I ~~took~~ borrowed some lines from your sublime legislation, found that
Exploring hands encountered no defence;

then ripped my pearls one from each ear
cast them into the churning water

an offering to the law of this river

here is the metaphor that knows no violence
and the Thames, fed with debris

Jug Jug
Chugachug

channelling the extremes of your imperial world
Prison and palace and reverberation

your poem, laying lines to separate land from her water
a title thirsty for mine

birthing the sound machine

*After Roald Dahl's 1949 'The Sound Machine', while
imperialism is collapsing, after the Second World War.*

they say humans can only
hear a bud bloom after the sound has been translated

flowers speak in a language we've termed
'hum' so when you hum to a flower it may choose to
open its petals or gaze at you

with pity. in this quest we can dwell in
imagination or build a machine to
amplify cells

the uncertainty: after the machine's invented
the flowers might just ignore you and keep on

humming, unintelligibly, with the flower next door
in Dahl's story all that matters

to Klausner, as he labours over his device, is whether he can
hear the sounds of roses being cut, can hear

the sound of a daisy as it's plucked from the ground, can really
hear the tree scream when hit with the axe. if, after

another war we forsake each modern mode of reproduction
    the phiii sssshhhhhhhhh the ttt-rrr-tt-rr-t-r and especially
the incessant budding

    we could spend a lifetime trying to translate the pain
a petal feels when plucked from a talking head

what hunters declare inevitable

the hunter watches his prey for twelve weeks
one through the internet eleven from his seat

before pointing two sentences
at the hunted's forehead

I love war
I love everything about it

shoulders tense as if recalling the moves that naturally follow such
declarations but this is not a time to die   the peace-war-peace-
war-peace-war cycle that hunters have declared inevitable around
more tables than she can imagine will not spin the hunted's head

the hunter's next bullet
looks bigger.   it ranks the hunted second in command

if this doesn't kill her the Sergeant surely will. Sergeants are nothing
if not executioners of the inevitable

the hunted sits with the gun pointing at her for 3 days (2 non-
working days included)

she practises slowing her heart beat considers whether to treat the
gun seriously like a machete that's turned breathing bodies into
piles of limbs or light like a feather quill

not a gun. an email.

after three days she looks at the

gun head on plucks the bullet from the screen tucks it into her
brainstem so she can recycle it whenever she wishes   peace-war-
peace-war-peace-peace-peace   hisses at the laptop

'the hunter is cunning but the hunter does not enjoy shooting the
deer when the deer refuses to run'   shrugs her shoulders to
release the tension

shuts the laptop down

FUSS OR FERTILISER

lullabies

at this hour, when tears spring and
lyrics curl octopus tentacles around
cylindrical torsos, the
  fights begin

to wake up in the middle
  of a strangling dream

to stuff the gaseous mid of night
  inside a chamber of soothing syllables

arrorró mi sol
arrorró mi sol arrorró pedazo
  de mi corazon

in this lullaby
  it no longer matters for
  whom I'm singing

for the hungry spirit
  for the unborn child

to cut a piece of one's heart
  and dissolve it   arrorró

through ventricles
  expanded by a mother's capacity for theft
  contracted by chambers of rhythm

at this hour, I understand that
Lilith has stolen the souls of children
    fewer nights than mothers have sung
    'begone you thief'

a father tongue

on Father's Day we go to
the local Italian restaurant

surrounded by families, mineral water and
gorgonzola gnocchi
we speculate

will you be fluent en Español, nuestra niño? hay no

I try to ask you this in Castellano but I
don't remember the word for 'fluent'

       perfectamente?   fluido?

you tell me in the language of love and invasion and uncertainty you're
not sure if that's the right word, it's not familiar   flu – ee – do

the promise of the tongue's invisible labour, the mind's reach for the
meanings folded away somewhere in the frontal lobe, that crinkly
squishy place between mouth and memory

spreading now, like breath, to fill the space between bites we begin to
argue over who'll do the work, make promises in the language of
law and invasion and certainty

I will learn new lullabies, arrorró mi niño, arrorró mi
amor, arrorró pedazo de mi corazón

and you? will unfurl your mother
tongue para tener una lengua nueva

Pronunciation Guide

Castellano → Cas-te-sha-no

Spanish–English translations:

en Español, nuestra nino? hay no

in Spanish, our baby? or not

arrorró mi niño
arrorró mi amor
arrorró pedazo de mi corazón

hush-a-bye my baby
hush-a-bye my love
hush-a-bye oh piece of my heart

para tener una lengua nueva

to father a new tongue (with feminine adjective and noun) or

to have a new tongue
(literal translation)

fuss or fertiliser

on the other side of the flyscreen window
   branches rasp against a saw

the dropped branches are collected and burnt
   small clouds of carbon dioxide rise from the pizza oven
   feed the garden through her leaves, I rise

to slide the window shut
   protect the lungs developing inside me

over east fires are burning

three and a half thousand kilometres away from the flames he wakes
   red-eyed with a need to prune and take cuttings

if it were me I'd have spent the time taking photos and collecting
   images like 'the blade's rust' to sprinkle on waxy waterproof leaves, for
      dramatic contrast   decay – growth!   burnt red – emerald green!

but your papa's decided we can't afford to keep
   fawning over the two flawless frangipani
   like parents we must prioritise things, now, that
      thrive without too much fuss or fertiliser

I walk carefully down the stairs out into the garden to announce
   smoke's coming into the bedroom

dreams of Eden have never looked so much like
   wielding a jagged instrument

of placenta and news

tiny legs keep hitting my insides

you're tumbling like a hungry seal into that lamplit hour in the
evening when I break the doctor's rules and lie flat on my back

your papa's watching your legs push my belly out
further into the world

go little one, gooooo
be gentle on your mum, little one, gentle

are you pedalling to get away from the drivers who refuse to
make eye contact with cyclists? are you learning how to

swim along the current of a fast-draining creek? are you already
marching to protest the rising price of water?

broken sentences filter through the closed wooden door

   fight fires refuse pay   Elders call police disarmed   no rain days

each word a stone sending ripples through the babbling stream inside me
we search again   *when does a foetus grow ears?*

imagine tiny folds of pale cartilage vibrating with truths that
travel faster than white noise

timekeeper

my body's keeping time
growth is the only change worth
noticing skin it turns out can expand without
bursting in ways balloons have only
imagined my nails grow fast I trim them in the courtyard
small crescent fertilisations of the
mulberry tree my
belly button is the most reliable
timekeeper of them all the shape that marks dermis-
barrier beginnings pushed by the
wriggly body below see it
 peeking out sinking in poking out before
settling into a small mound softer even than a
a writer's fingertips or
the womb my belly beats an
evensong of afternoon – a chance now to
hear petals fall on concrete – my relaxin-flooded
hips thrum of late evening no chance left
to worship leisurely walks or fear
extreme UV levels but how long can growth remain the measurement
when my belly button retreats to the place where it
began someone else will define
time for me I'll cede my
stretched skin to gravity and watch
change turn loose

I offered advice

at every
chance
about
the art
of
vomiting
on nature
strips
I
acted
as though this
world
is full of
people
breathing in
oxygen to
saturate
more than
one body's
bloodstream at once

common sense
descended from
above like a
Truman
Show voiceover
children are expensive
time is of
the essence

silence
will soon be
memory

I conducted a
conversation with
a minus-4-day-old
cluster
of
rapidly
dividing cells I
listened to

sound like it was
an ocean of hands
pressing at the
small of my
back I
reacted
to music
like
it was pure
vibration
I sang about
a hero
who
comes along
whenever
someone
asked for the
baby's gender I

read enough
experts
on

freedom
to understand that
it is opposite to
breath it

starts in
the mind then
travels
along
melodies
ancestors
out through the
mouth

seeing Bougainvillea

it was named after Louis-Antoine de Bougainville but
Jeanne Baret probably saw this plant before he did

its trunk all twisted as truth tended to be in those days its
petals so delicate they must have been passed through the mill

Baret was de Bougainville's lover, his assistant Baret was an
expert in botany, she flattened her breasts with linen bandages to become

'the first European woman to travel the globe'

in Walyalup, the bougainvillea flowers for most of the year except when,
in the depths of makuru, season of rain and fertility, the
weather turns cold and

luminescent carpets become floral spectacles, a deciduous kind of rest

pink petals

by the fourth oestrogen injection
I look down to the needle, then look up

pink flowers in the courtyard

how can I tell you about
the difference between these flowers and this needle, the
point and the petals

how can I tell you about
the pink outside
rosy ruddy blushing raw approaching red but never being red

how can I tell you
about the needle
approaching my skin, entering my abdomen easily

how can I tell you about the difference between these two things
in the morning's shadows and spectres

the soft and the sharp the warm translucent life and
the cool opaque metal yes, the blooms, and yes, the prick

how can I tell you it's not sexy but it is reproductive

dear, dear bougainvillea

how can I tell you the pink is not of some generic female called 'girl'
is not a point is supple rosy roar

spectres of history

my womb was a spectre hovering, amorphous, over sovereign land and
from my womb this process was continuing this conversion of souls and
bodies into wide-eyed dolls can I interrupt this process for long enough
to peel my womb away from the land is it enough to name my son Juan
instead of John (there are enough dolls named John already)

before John there was umbilical cord there was bilya there was placenta
there was egg there was no need to check how far my womb had spread
no need to ask whether I am person or doll mother or child womb or
biological weapon

woman, womb, fire

I've never seen my follicles before or

held a clipboard in my palm
making marks to record their size

   1.2 1.7 1.1

I try not to make comparisons

  is that normal? I ask
  what's normal says the nurse

after a while she turns to me
  yes she says *it's more than average*

I, too, had stored pride in my potential
  but now potential looks complex

a follicle? *a dry fruit derived from a single carpel that
  opens on one side only to release its seeds*

a small secretory cavity, sac, or gland
  the sheath of cells and connective tissue which surrounds the root of a hair

I have in my body *small spherical or vase-like groups of cells enclosing a
  cavity in which some other structure grows or other
  material is contained*

a cavity inside which I tuck conversations, petals of bougainvillea, flames
of the fires you lovingly light for me, flames that leap like there's
  nothing left to seek but fuel

I mumble under my breath *so life is turning out like this* the
  beauty of a grainy image, cute flammable figures all in a row

zygote

the conception was special

it began in a
room we never entered

in a perfectly circular
transparent dish

sperm and egg
became zygote

it took a lab coat
careful measurements

a superbly steady hand

at this stage of the process
you begin to believe

Adam-and-Eve were not invented by God
Adam-and-Eve were invented by scientists

for in the beginning you were zygote
kept safe by the sterility of polystyrene

and the two spirits that floated above the dish

keeping watch over
cells that exceed their structures

having travelled from their places of work
two and five suburbs distant

respectively

wanted!

the need for a

virile stock to

propagate the generations to come is particularly

urgent

unless steps are taken to ensure the

perpetuation of a

healthy and

normal population

before it is too late

we will be inviting

inevitable

shipwreck

as a people.

Lorna Hodgkinson, Superintendent of the Education of Mental Defectives, 1923 (evidence to the New South Wales Royal Commission on Lunacy Law and Administration, 1923, p. 660).

how fleshy they look to me

now might be the time to look at a child and cry

she's curled in her mother's lap, her mother stroking her hair
her mother's speaking with her mother

I wonder if they realise how fleshy they look to me how much their love
speaks of the number of times skin cells divide in three generations
(around 3 times 10 to the power of 16)

in this grief, my respect for people grows every day by which I mean my
respect for the number of scars hidden under the clothes around me
grows, every day

in this grief I fail to understand why we're still walking round in
neat skins and folded limbs, why we haven't gone down to
the Derbarl Yerrigan yet and

turned, all of us, butterfly to cocoon, whimpering mammal to tidal wail

since scar is protein in random realignment and heart is protein, blood, and
patterns and grief is pretending to do important stuff while
we realign we could

let our pearly shifting cells move to the offerings of the Boorloo sun

I'm here to keep you warm you while you change

Day 3 or Day 1510 or Day something

these days are more full of vomit,
women's magazines and
peace than they have been for a while

we say simply things like
it's out of our hands? *it's out of our bodies*

mid-morning they call me up, tell
us we've got 10 embryos

the dish is in a room we
have never been in *wonder*
what they call that room

where they keep the embryos
probably 'embryo room'

we laugh louder and longer
than it warrants and

my stomach hurts
jabbed, penetrated, more than 10 times

the doctor tells us
these anti-nausea tablets

are the same they use for chemo

and again, pregnancy seems like it could
so easily slip and slide into disease

the truths are as plain as toast and
seasonless two minutes noodles

how volatile the body's systems
how close are you to me

the prettiest

The history of IVF has long entwined its sweaty fingers with that of eugenics. The man whose research informed IVF technology, Sir Francis Galton, argued that non-physical traits are hereditary. His 1896 book was called Hereditary Genius. *It informed Nazi policy. In*
1963 the University College London renamed The Francis Galton Laboratory for National Eugenics as The Galton Laboratory of
the Department of Human Genetics and
Biometry. Our doctor is a
woman a celebrity
fertility specialist, so we're told, but on D-day
the doctor is a man and we are not prepared for the
number of people present at this
immaculate conception

they

tell us

   we choose the prettiest embryo

      suddenly

      a history of unnatural selection

      inside me

WATCHING *FREE WILLY* IN THE AGE OF COVID-19

the freeze

soon after I enter the hospital
midwives and   anaesthetists
gather around me as if   I've
become nothing less vital than
a city's spire, or a ship's   mast

the feeling doesn't surprise me
for what is giving birth if not a
chance to become   important
after the second hour I   look
into the eyes of the lead midwife
and ask something like

    is it even possible?

she grips my hand

   what d'you usually do to relax darling?

   breathe deep, like in yoga

but breath will not move me past
a pain that has no address in   this
limb or that organ my   relaxin-
flooded body is a wave   crashing
on itself I scream as if my life might
be frozen forever in this mutation

my imperatives travel through the

ward suggesting to the labourer   in
the next room she too should clutch
a Hydralyte icy pole in her   burning
fist know that you can
melt death before it melts you

nervous

outside, morning breaks
a promise of light daring me to lift my lids

inside, sunlight scrubs window rims
glass frosting runs to syrup

my mind rests in the folds of stripy crimson curtains while
two-sided towelling cloths perch, ballerinas en pointe, on
the towering bassinet stage

my nervous system hasn't learnt to respond to your notes
of desire, pitched, but without a definite meaning

I, sit up, lie down, sit up, lie down

until the nervous system starts to remember a time when there was no
want to sink into first light like it's an endless pancake no

need to question if the liquid necessities of life will dry up no
need to bury urgent instructions in the feeding troughs of night

outside, the Indian Ocean whips the
air into a frenzy

inside, I lift my arm toward the ceiling
find I can take hold of the closest ray of the sun

matrescence

of course, land has been ocean for ages and yet people continue to
speak about us as if we're solid objects one of those carved wooden
statues of a mother nursing her child inviting touch merely by its
form we sit outside at the café, to be safe, and because the freedom
and frequency of scooters on South Freo's Marine Terrace reminds
me of Naarm because most things these days remind me of Naarm
except for this woman before me who

pauses to stare at my chest before she greets me and even then that's
only because I've never breastfed in Naarm I smile wide with dagger
eyes at this woman ashamed of how nervous I am that a stare might
lead to touch while everyone else seems to want to draw closer to life
after restrictions lift they embrace each

other in the morning queue as if they did not see the look in the
doctor's eyes when she prescribed an antibiotic not proven to be
effective for mastitis but preferable to risking hospitalisation when
someone approaches I hold you still but not as still as a statue

I dream of a carefully spaced village where disease is an object of
curiosity and we greet each other with questions that allow us to be
land then ocean then land again before we even step through the
front door hello, sister, over there, how strong is your fear today

Watching *Free Willy* with a Newborn in the Age of Covid-19

Will you ever watch a movie knowing America as a waking dream?

Will you question why animals have passports?

Will you know how training an animal can be a form of healing

    and so can giving up your ambitions to discipline him?

Will you know that small healings are worthy of big screens?

Will you know much of the ocean?

Will you consider inheriting her spray, and all her writhing creatures?

Will you question if water is yours to inherit?

Will you study how fast diseases can jump between species?

Will you know how love, too, can jump between species, and live

    as large in the traps of glass tanks as in the crashing freedom of waves?

Settlers swim in Wadawurrung water Whadjuk water

Here, we celebrate that we are, toward the end of our brief history, still visitors. The caravan wheels are chocked for the summer. My grandfather wakes at sunrise to sit on the pier and watch the tides rise and fall. Rod in hand, bucket at feet. He skins his catch in the caravan annex. There's nowhere to hide from the smell. Nana crumbs and fries the fillet. Golden fruit of the sea. Oil running into carefully folded paper towel. Crinkle-cut potato fries in the pan.

We swim until our bathers are scratchy with sand. When the sun dips, we shower in the cubicle with sisters and cousins and laugh at the clumps of green and brown plants stuck to our bellies. The fresh hot water is bliss. Not because it's fresh and hot but because it's a sting-less imitation of the salt river-meets-ocean water we've reluctantly left for the day.

Years later, three hundred and fifty thousand kilometres west, on another Country, my mother and my out-laws and my love and I play in the Indian Ocean. After, we lie on grass to air-dry then drive inland, to a new home, and laugh about the piles of sand tucked into bathers. We dump them onto the bathroom floor, messy unplanned sandcastles. Our laughter showers us with childhood, the place where land and sea do not need to be the same thing, do not need to be gentle, do not need to submit to each other, in order to exist in the same word.

A disease is spreading, unevenly, across the world and there's something bigger than Australia about swimming together in this ocean (highway to England, back road to Montevideo). We struggle to push nostalgia down. It's so buoyant now, always bobbing on the mind's surface. The caravan. The pier. The seaweed clinging to belly. The nostalgia floats until the next wave arrives.

'Beach' visits me here, over and again, rocks me, foetus, to sleep.

Assisted reproduction

they say that by 2045 most couples might need
    'just a little help from science'

when a friend explains to her child what
IVF means she says something like
    it's when a couple can't have a baby naturally so a
    baby is made with help from science

I wonder, then, if my baby, dressed in all natural
fibres, carries the scent of a petri dish
    we begin in the ocean
    we continue, sprouting seedlings, in labs

I don't know if I want my family to be a walking billboard for IVF

I do know that my baby's cheeks are soft and they smell floral to me, like
perfection, like the kind of creature who turns its head to check if you
agree that we should keep

jumping up and down in doctors' waiting rooms because it feels amazing

they also say something other than age is affecting childbearing in
particular, phthalates, used to make plastic soft and flexible are
    'of paramount concern'

    and that these rapidly dividing cells are extra sensitive but they don't
    clarify whether that's because they're small or only
        because they're dividing

the apocalypse birthed by us

this summer pumps a record heat

   we lose track of how many days scream above

40 degrees Celsius when we start to implode in the way

       stars implode once they start to run out of fuel in the way parents

implode after sleeping for months with eyes and hearts

    wide open you perform the only act able to cool this

burning relationship down you buy a rubber paddling

     pool then you step away from my sweaty

pits and swim a twinkle across your dry eye the next

      day second day of a lockdown fires rage in the hills people

flee homes ash rains down drifts across the surface of the pool our faces

       lift greet vagrant particles of grey it's never been so

clear we're making life from life right here please dear future let us

     understand how you can taste bitter fire and arrive all easy

                rain

something specific about this boodja

'Something universal this way you become'
– Aditi Machado, 'Then', 2019.

I try to pause systematically before I drop you at childcare

on the way to the car we watch pearly dew slide along the
leaves of a debatably toxic shrub, the father in me
wanting you to love the leaves as much as you love risk the
mother in me wanting to keep you
far away from all things remotely poisonous as if
it's possible to separate imported trees from care from
trips to the children's hospital where
an Australian family is still demanding to hear why their daughter's
case was not escalated why not all bodies appear equal in
this story why not all suburbs are built from the clay that lies beneath them

tomorrow I'll find a way to explain to you why you
should stay suspicious of rules that pertain to keep
planets from colliding but ignore the way it's impossible
to separate gravity from movement
from breath

sweetheart there are celestial bodies there are living breathing bodies,
there are bodies marked for immediate medical attention

in the
    car I sing you twinkle twinkle en Castellano wondering if it's
        familiar to you yet taking pleasure in three minutes of
deviance from
        this colony's language sure you must hear in my elastic
    vowels the way Castellano has yet to travel from my tongue through
my belly button into the evenly spaced grammar of my spine sure you can
    hear that this language neither belongs to the boodja speeding
beneath us

  estrellita, donde estas?
  quiero verte titilar

        at the traffic lights we stop

two stars

        held close to earth only by seat belts burn our specific selves
    high above the warmed clay bricks of Maylands

Susannah on the Deck

below deck, the judge was tapping his wooden justice against her
forehead again

    tat tat   tat tat   she tried to ignore him to focus on

coordinating the tilt of her arm with the purse of her
baby's round lips the feat of gathering every string and cord in
her body to fulfill this creature's base needs

once drained, she places her sleeping
daughter beside the father and
comes up here to glimpse the
underside that place where things live without apology
slimy plankton pointy urchins hungry

sharks she's heard of the country toward which she's
propelled she imagines it runs according to rules
different from those at home it
comforts her, now, the ocean with its own rules
appetites, bites, digestions, expulsions, each weed subject to
change without notice

up here on the deck she's
far from land's gavels until a run of
blood dribbles down her inner thigh and she
sees what lives beneath her skirt two legs about to
carry her through the force of
a long beginning

this place called mother

I drape my limbs across soft slats

allow early winter sun to melt the thoughts off my face let them
run into my hairline, trickle along my chin listen to the

neighbour's swimming pool pump grind the
solid plans of afternoon into the free-floating dust of evening take

slow sips of a prebiotic carbonated drink
clumsy, I spill it, unsure whether I'm too

tired to move or whether this is the time of life to give oneself over to
the small pleasure of icy liquid blooming, the ways

skin is only a border until it's not

arms wrapped across my chin the
drink floods my stockings while

body anchors body
all the childless versions of me begin to flow

drench this place called mother

Author Note and References

Many of these poems are based on archival and published research. This collection presents versions of history that carry truth but are neither final nor definitive. I have used informed imagination to connect with the past, mediated by records, places, intuition, conversations, and the body, as well as by my learnt knowledge of colonial processes and structures.

The image on page eight is of the entry titled 'O'Brien, Susannah (c. 1763–1846)', Australian Dictionary of Biography Online, peopleaustralia.anu.edu.au/biography/obrien-susannah-31631.

Numerous poems draw on research published in Sian Rees, *The Floating Brothel: The Extraordinary True Story of an 18th-Century Ship and Its Cargo of Female Convicts*, Hachette, 2001.

'the midwife' quotes one Dr Bland, quoted in Sian Rees, *The Floating Brothel*, p. 176.

'this prisoner' is informed by Joy Damousi's 'Beyond the "Origins Debate": Theorising Sexuality and Gender Disorder in Convict Women's History', *Australian Historical Studies*, vol. 27, 1966, pp. 59–71.

'Federation pains' draws on Marilyn Lake's 'Mission Impossible: How Men Gave Birth to the Australian Nation – Nationalism, Gender and Other Seminal Acts', *Gender & History*, vol. 4, no. 3, 1992; It also draws on research in Clare Wright's *You Daughters of Freedom: The Australians Who Won the Vote and Inspired the World*, Text Publishing, 2019.

'These women are the great, great grandmothers of thousands of Australians today' is a quote from 'Convict Stunt Commemorated', *The Sydney Morning Herald*, 18 June 2004, www.smh.com.au/national/convict-stunt-commemorated-20040618-gdj5c4.html.

It responds to the image, *A Flash Mob: A Singular Act of Female Rebellion in Van Diemen's Land*, 1844.

'Waste Land' includes the lines 'Looking into the heart of light, the silence', 'Exploring hands encounter no defence', and 'Prison and palace and reverberation' from T.S. Eliot, 'The Waste Land', 1922. It also references the Victorian *Waste Lands Act* (1842), for 'regulating the sale of Waste Land in the Australian colonies', digitalcollections.qut.edu.au/4668/

'more than one body's bloodstream' references Bobbi Sykes' lines 'We do not always talk / of our pregnancy / for we are pregnant / with the thrust of freedom' in the poem 'Cycle', from *Love Poems and Other Revolutionary Actions*, Cammeray Saturday Centre, 1979. It also references the lyrics of 'Hero' by Mariah Carey and Walter Afanasieff, 1993.

'birthing the sound machine' references Roald Dahl's 'The Sound Machine', *The New Yorker*, 17 September 1949.

'what the hunter declares inevitable' responds to Marilyn Chin's lines 'It's not the hunter who is cunning / But the hunted who has learnt' in 'First Lessons Redux' in *The Phoenix Gone, The Terrace Empty*, Milkweed, 2009.

'a history of Oysters in the sea near where I was born' references Lewis Caroll's 'The Walrus and the Carpenter' in *Through the Looking-Glass*, MacMillan & Co Ltd, 1871.

'it is not as a woman' is a paraphrase and re-imagination of the admission speech to Western Australian Parliament made by Senator Dorothy Tangney on 24 September 1943, Parliament of Australia, aph.gov.au/About_Parliament/Parliamentary_Departments/Parliamentary_Library/Publications_Archive/archive/women/43Tangney. The phrase 'it is not as a woman' is a direct quote from Tangney's speech.

Claire G. Coleman, 'Apocalypses are more than the stuff of fiction – First Nations Australians survived one', ABC Radio National, 8 December 2017, abc.net.au/news/2017-12-08/first-nations-australians-survived-an-apocalypse-says-author/9224026.

Numerous of these poems were written in the space of 'archival poetics' theorised and realised by First Nations poets, including but not limited to Charmaine Papertalk Green, Alison Whittaker, Elfie Shiosaki and Natalie Harkin.

Acknowledgements

This book was written and published on stolen lands. I wish to acknowledge the unceded sovereignty of the Whadjuk people of the Noongar nation, of the Wathauwurrung people, of the Wurundjeri and Boon Wurrung peoples of the Kulin confederation, and of all First Nations people across the world. I acknowledge that as a white settler woman I'm a beneficiary of the ongoing crimes of colonisation.

Thank you to the many friends, colleagues and students whose passion for histories has buoyed me; especially, to Elfie Shiosaki for your wisdom and support, and for widening paths for us to write from the heart, and to Emily Sun for your friendship and our conversations. Thank you to Talya Rubin, Annette Orr, Judith Huang, Kimberly Minerva, Miriam Wei Wei Lo, Brieanna Collard and N'Gadie Roberts for sharing spaces of poetry-making. Thank you to Tracey Banivanua Mar for alerting me to the false separation between land and water, and for all you taught us.

Thank you to Mildred and to Margaret for teaching me how to earth strikes of lightning and the importance of keeping memories alive. Thank you to my family, especially Sue, Kirsty, Graeme, Lyn, Monica and Luis for your care and support beyond borders. Thank you to Esteban for watering the lemon tree while I edited, for sharing my yearning for colonies to be a thing of the past, and for your love. Gracias para Thiago for making our lives abundant with laughter and promise. I hope you read these poems with interest someday and know that your origins are so much richer than this book.

Thank you to the Perth and Melbourne poetry communities for keeping us alive and connected. Thank you to Melinda Smith for giving feedback on early versions of some of these poems. Thank you to the editors of the following publications where some of these poems first appeared: The Blue Nib, Scum, Portside Review, Westerly Magazine, Australian Multilingual Writing Project, Authora Australis and Cordite Poetry Review, and especially to editors Nadia Niaz, Elfie Shiosaki, Robert Wood, Linda Martin, Laura Keenan, Ella Kurz, Simone King, Claire Delahunty, Kate Pickard and Terri-ann White.

Sincere thanks to Lisa Gorton for your insights and careful attention to detail in editing this collection. Thank you to Georgia Richter and the team at Fremantle Press for all your work, trust and support. Any mistakes are my own.

A version of 'Settler Dawns' was shortlisted for the Flash the Cover Competition, published on Writing WA website, 2020. It is inspired by the cover of False Claims of Colonial Thieves, by Charmaine Papertalk Green and John Kinsella, Magabala Books, 2018.

'pink petals' first published in Nadia Rhook, boots, UWA Publishing, 2020.

'Broome speak' and 'Oyster interrupted' first published in The Blue Nib, January 2020.

'a father tongue' first published in the Australian Multilingual Writing Project, January 2020.

'timekeeper' first published in Ella Kurz, Simone King and Claire Delahunty, eds, What We Carry: Poetry on Childbearing, Recent Work Press, 2021.

A version of a section of 'origins' was published in Authora Australis, July 2021.

'something specific about this boodja' was published in Westerly Magazine, vol. 66, no. 2, November 2021.

'Settlers in Wadawurrung Water Whadjuk Water' and a version of 'in her wake' were published in *Portside Review*, December 2021.

'the midwife' was published in *Cordite Poetry Review*, February 2022.

Nadia Rhook is a non-Indigenous poet and historian, born in Naarm (Melbourne) and currently living in Boorloo (Perth). She has a PhD in History from La Trobe University and lectures in History and Indigenous Studies at The University of Western Australia. Nadia has published widely on linguistic and medical histories of south-east Australia and is interested in creative translations of history. She curated the heritage exhibition *Moving Tongues: Language and Migration in 1890s Melbourne*, and designed the public walking tour *Migration Melbourne*. Her poetry appears in various journals and anthologies including *Cordite Poetry Review, Peril Magazine, Mascara Literary Review, Westerly Magazine, The Enchanting Verses Literary Review, Portside Review* and *What We Carry: Poetry on Childbearing* (Recent Work Press). Nadia's first collection, *boots*, was released by UWA Publishing early in 2020, weeks before she became a pandemic parent. *Second Fleet Baby* is her second poetry collection.

Also available

A collection that speaks of the roar inside the woman, these poems are structured around a suite of Frida Kahlo paintings. They are love poems, poems of tenderness and anger, queer passion and fulfilment, and maternal gratitude – a powerful way of healing, of reclaiming the past, and of embracing the beauty of now.

'Erotic, feminist, sensitive and skilled, Bateman is a poet who wants, and deserves, to be widely read.' – *Saturday Age*

fremantlepress.com.au

from Fremantle Press

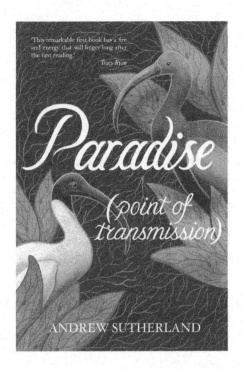

This brilliant debut collection examines a 'haunted' Queer and HIV-positive identity, and follows an HIV diagnosis and departure from Singapore, when Andrew Sutherland returned to Perth, the city of his birth.

'Full of Queer feeling and thinking, these poems are frank, moving, ironic, dazzling and confronting; playful, yet at the same time serious. Their spirited imagination and intelligence transform whatever they encounter, whether in personal or wider social experience, or drawing on ancient myth and contemporary popular culture – because "a touch of genre helps the silences stay Camp".' – *Tracy Ryan*

and all good bookstores

First published 2022 by
Fremantle Press Inc. trading as Fremantle Press
PO Box 158, North Fremantle, Western Australia, 6159
fremantlepress.com.au

Cover image from The Miriam and Ira D. Wallach Division of Art, Prints
and Photographs: Print Collection, The New York Public Library. 'Plate
XLV: Delesseria sinuosa, Lamour' NYPL Digital Collections.
digitalcollections.nypl.org/items/84a79560-0070-0136-37c0-2b71ac269dcc
Cover design by Carolyn Brown, tendeersigh.com.au
Printed and bound by IPG

A catalogue record for this
book is available from the
National Library of Australia

NATIONAL
LIBRARY
OF AUSTRALIA

ISBN: 9781760991692 (paperback)
ISBN 9781760991708 (ebook)

Department of
Local Government, Sport
and Cultural Industries

GOVERNMENT OF
WESTERN AUSTRALIA

lotterywest

Fremantle Press is supported by the State Government through the
Department of Local Government, Sport and Cultural Industries.

Fremantle Press respectfully acknowledges the Whadjuk people of the
Noongar nation as the Traditional Owners and Custodians of the land
where we work in Walyalup.